AWESOME ANIMALS IN THEIR HABITATS

PROTECTING WETLAND ANIMALS

LAUREN KUKLA

Consulting Editor, Diane Craig, M.A./Reading Specialist

Sandcastle

An Imprint of Abdo Publishing
abdopublishing.com

abdopublishing.com

Published by Abdo Publishing, a division of ABDO, PO Box 398166, Minneapolis, Minnesota 55439. Copyright © 2017 by Abdo Consulting Group, Inc. International copyrights reserved in all countries. No part of this book may be reproduced in any form without written permission from the publisher. SandCastle™ is a trademark and logo of Abdo Publishing.

Printed in the United States of America, North Mankato, Minnesota

102016
012017

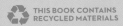
Editor: Rebecca Felix
Content Developer: Nancy Tuminelly
Cover and Interior Design and Production: Mighty Media, Inc.
Photo Credits: Featureflash Photo Agency/Shutterstock Images, Shutterstock Images

Publisher's Cataloging-in-Publication Data

Names: Kukla, Lauren, author.
Title: Protecting wetland animals / by Lauren Kukla.
Description: Minneapolis, MN : Abdo Publishing, 2017. | Series: Awesome
   animals in their habitats
Identifiers: LCCN 2016944682 | ISBN 9781680784305 (lib. bdg.) |
   ISBN 9781680797831 (ebook)
Subjects: LCSH: Animals--Habitations--Juvenile literature. | Habitat (Ecology)--
   Juvenile literature. | Wildlife conservation--Juvenile literature.
Classification: DDC 577--dc23
LC record available at http://lccn.loc.gov/2016944682

SandCastle™ Level: Transitional

SandCastle™ books are created by a team of professional educators, reading specialists, and content developers around five essential components—phonemic awareness, phonics, vocabulary, text comprehension, and fluency—to assist young readers as they develop reading skills and strategies and increase their general knowledge. All books are written, reviewed, and leveled for guided reading, early reading intervention, and Accelerated Reader™ programs for use in shared, guided, and independent reading and writing activities to support a balanced approach to literacy instruction. The SandCastle™ series has four levels that correspond to early literacy development. The levels are provided to help teachers and parents select appropriate books for young readers.

EMERGING · BEGINNING · TRANSITIONAL · FLUENT

CONTENTS

ABOUT WETLANDS

Wetlands are places where
shallow water covers land.

They are home to many plants and
animals.

Frogs live in wetlands.
So do turtles and snails.

Birds live in wetlands.

They eat fish
and bugs.

Some wetlands are near oceans.
These have salt water.

Crabs live in saltwater wetlands.
They **burrow** in mud.

Crocodiles live in some saltwater wetlands.

Steve Irwin was a **conservationist**. He worked to **protect** crocodiles.

Many wetlands have fresh water.

Newts live in these wetlands. So do beavers. Beavers build dams.

Wetlands are in danger.
Pollution harms them.

Humans cover wetlands.
They build houses and roads.

Wetlands are important **habitats**. Many animals have their babies there.

Wetland plants
clean the water.

We must work to **protect** wetlands. You can help!

Pick up any trash you see. Don't let
lawn **chemicals** run into wetlands.

THINK ABOUT IT

Have you ever visited a wetland?
What animals did you see?

GLOSSARY

burrow – to dig a tunnel or a hole in the ground.

chemical – something that reacts or changes when mixed with something else.

conservationist – a person who works to save or protect something.

habitat – the area or environment where a person or animal usually lives.

newt – a small salamander with short legs that lives on land and in water.

pollution – contamination of the air, water, or soil caused by man-made waste.

protect – to guard someone or something from harm or danger.

shallow – not deep.